THE BUCK STOPS WITH ME

10 WAYS TO TAKE CONTROL OF YOUR LIFE

RANJEET SINGH

Made with ♥ on the Notion Press Platform
www.notionpress.com

To my father, Late Ghanshyam Singh,

Who taught me the true meaning of ownership and responsibility.

You were the first to step beyond the fields into the unknown world of the service sector, carving a path where none existed before. Your courage to embrace challenges, commitment to taking responsibility, and unwavering belief in hard work have shaped who I am today. You showed me that life's journey is built on choices, integrity, and the willingness to step up, no matter how uncertain the road ahead.

This book is a tribute to your legacy—a reflection of the values you lived by and the lessons you instilled in me.

Thank you for leading the way.

Contents

Preface

I wasn't always someone who took full responsibility for my life. In fact, for years, I blamed my circumstances, other people, and even luck for the things that weren't going the way I wanted. If my job weren't fulfilling, I'd tell myself it was because the company wasn't offering me enough opportunities. If my relationships weren't working out, I'd find reasons to fault the other person. And when my health started to suffer, I chalked it up to being "too busy" to take care of myself.

But then, something changed. One day, as I was sitting in the middle of yet another frustrating situation, I had a realisation that stopped me: the common denominator in all of these challenges was me. My choices, actions (or inactions), and mindset played a far bigger role in my life than I had ever realised. The more I reflected on this, the clearer it became. I had been handing over the steering wheel of my life to circumstances and other people when, in fact, I was the one who should have been driving all along.

From that moment on, I consciously decided to take full responsibility for my life—every aspect of it. My career, relationships, health, finances, and personal growth came down to one fundamental truth: the buck stops with me. And once I embraced that truth, everything changed. I stopped waiting for the world to hand me what I wanted and started creating the life I envisioned.

This book is the culmination of my journey, filled with lessons that have empowered me to recognize the immense power we all possess when we choose to take control of our lives. I've penned these insights for you, the reader, ready to steer your life's course. Whether you're feeling trapped in your career, grappling with relationships, concerned about your finances, or simply seeking more purpose, I'm here to reveal that the power to transform it is within your grasp.

I'll share my personal stories, both the challenges and the triumphs, and provide actionable steps to initiate meaningful changes today. You'll understand that taking charge of your life isn't just about shouldering the blame when things go awry; it's about realizing your potential to make different choices and shape your future.

I want to be clear: this journey isn't about perfection. You won't have everything figured out overnight, and that's okay. What matters is that you begin. Start small, stay committed, and watch how the ripple effect of responsibility transforms every area of your life.

Are you prepared to seize control?
Are you ready to cease waiting for change and start instigating it?
If your answer is yes, then this book is your guide.

Let's get started—because the buck stops with you.

With gratitude and anticipation for your journey,

- Ranjeet Singh

CHAPTER ONE

The Choice Compass: Steering Life in the Direction You Want

I still remember the day when I truly understood the power of responsibility. It wasn't a grand vision or a life-altering event but a simple moment that shifted my perspective entirely.

I sat at my kitchen table, staring at a stack of unpaid bills and an endless to-do list. I felt overwhelmed, frustrated, and stuck. For the longest time, I had been blaming my circumstances—my demanding job, the economy, even bad luck—for the state of my life. But as I sat there that day, I thought: *What if I stopped blaming everything else and started taking responsibility for where I was?*

That single thought changed everything.

Understanding Responsibility
At its core, responsibility is about owning your actions and their outcomes. It's about recognising that while you can't

control everything that happens to you, you can control how you respond. It's the understanding that your choices, big and small, shape your life.

For a long time, I thought responsibility was a heavy burden that meant more work and stress. But I've come to realise that responsibility is liberating. When you take responsibility, you take control. You move from being a passive participant in your life to an active creator of your future.

Think about it this way: every time you blame something or someone else for where you are in life—your job, your financial situation, or even your relationships—you're essentially saying, "I have no control over this." It's like handing over the keys to your life to someone else and letting them drive while you sit in the passenger seat, just along for the ride. But here's the thing: you can't decide where to go if you're not driving. You're reacting to wherever the road takes you, which can feel frustrating or even hopeless.

I used to do this all the time. When things didn't go my way, I'd blame my boss for not recognising my hard work, the economy for making it hard to save money, or even my friends for not understanding me. It felt easier to point the finger at something external because it meant I didn't have to deal with the uncomfortable truth that maybe, just maybe, I could have done something differently.

But here's the kicker: when you're always blaming something outside yourself, you're giving away your power. You're saying, "I'm not in control of my life; these external factors are." And as long as you believe that, nothing will change. You'll stay stuck in the same place, feeling frustrated and powerless.

Now, imagine flipping that script. What if, instead of blaming external factors, you asked yourself, "What can I do differently?" This is where the magic happens. When you stop blaming and start taking responsibility, you take back the keys to your life. You become the driver again, and suddenly, the possibilities open up.

Let me give you a real-life example from my own experience. There was a time when I felt completely stuck in my career. I was working hard, doing everything I thought was right, but I wasn't getting promoted, and my salary wasn't increasing the way I wanted. Naturally, I blamed my boss. I thought, "He doesn't see my potential. He's holding me back." This mindset led to resentment and frustration, and honestly, it made me miserable at work.

But then, I had a moment of clarity. I realised that as long as I blamed my boss, I was stuck waiting for him to change. And what if he never did? Was I going to stay in this unhappy place forever? That's when I decided to take responsibility for my career. I asked myself, "What can I do to change my situation?"

I started looking at my actions. Was I truly giving my best, or was I doing the minimum because I felt unappreciated? Was I clearly communicating my goals to my boss, or did I assume he knew what I wanted? Was I seeking opportunities to grow or waiting for them to be handed to me?

These questions were uncomfortable, but they were necessary. I realised that there were things within my control that I hadn't been addressing. So, I made a plan. I began taking on more challenging projects, even if they weren't assigned to me. I started having open conversations with my boss about my career goals and asking for feedback on improving. I also began investing in my development by taking courses and reading books related to my field.

The change didn't happen overnight, but over time, it did. I started to see growth in my career. I felt more engaged at work, and eventually, promotions and salary increases followed. But the most important change was in how I felt about myself. I no longer felt like a victim of circumstance. I felt empowered because I had taken control of my destiny.

This shift in mindset—from blaming external factors to taking responsibility—was transformative. It taught me that I have the power to create different outcomes in my life. And you do too.

When you accept responsibility, you're not just admitting that you could have done something differently; you're acknowledging that you have the power to do something differently in the future. It's about recognising that while you can't control everything, you can control how you respond. And in that response lies your power.

So, the next time you find yourself blaming something or someone else for your situation, take a moment to pause. Ask yourself, "What can I do to change this?" Even if the change is small, it's a step towards reclaiming your power and taking control of your life. Trust me; that feeling of empowerment is worth every bit of discomfort that comes with taking responsibility.

The Shift from Victim to Leader

One of the most profound changes that comes with taking responsibility is the shift in mindset from victim to leader. When you see yourself as a victim, you feel helpless and powerless. You believe that life happens to you and you can do little about it. This mindset leads to frustration, resentment, and often, inaction.

On the other hand, when you see yourself as the leader of your life, you feel empowered. You recognise that while you can't control everything, you can control your responses, decisions, and actions. This mindset fosters confidence, resilience, and proactive behaviour.

I experienced this shift firsthand. Once I started taking responsibility for my life, I began to see opportunities where before I saw obstacles. I started making decisions aligned with my goals and values rather than just reacting to circumstances. This proactive approach positively changed my career, relationships, and overall well-being.

The Benefits of Embracing Responsibility

Embracing responsibility brings numerous benefits that can enhance every aspect of your life. Here are some of the most impactful ones:

1. Increased Confidence
When you take responsibility for your life, you build trust

in yourself and your abilities. You prove to yourself that you can handle challenges and make things happen. This confidence spills over into all areas of your life, making you more willing to take on new challenges and pursue your goals.

2. Better Decision-Making

Owning your choices forces you to think more carefully about them. You become more deliberate and thoughtful, considering the potential consequences and aligning your decisions with your long-term goals. This leads to better outcomes and fewer regrets.

3. Improved Relationships

Taking responsibility in your interactions leads to healthier, more fulfilling relationships. You're more likely to communicate openly, apologise when wrong, and work collaboratively to solve problems. Others will respect and trust you more, knowing you stand by your words and actions.

4. Greater Resilience

Life is full of ups and downs, but when you take responsibility, you're better equipped to handle adversity. You see challenges as opportunities to learn and grow rather than unbeatable obstacles. This resilience helps you bounce back from setbacks and keep moving forward.

5. Enhanced Personal Growth

Responsibility is a catalyst for personal development. By owning your experiences, you gain valuable insights into your strengths, weaknesses, values, and aspirations. This self-awareness is key to continuous growth and self-improvement.

How to Start Taking Responsibility

Embracing responsibility is a journey that starts with small, everyday actions. Here are some practical steps to help you begin:

1. Acknowledge Your Role

In any situation, pause and consider your role. Ask yourself, "What choices did I make that led to this outcome?" Be honest with yourself, even if it's uncomfortable. Recognising your part is the first step toward making positive changes.

2. Stop Blaming Others

It's easy to point fingers when things go wrong, but blame only keeps you stuck. Instead, focus on what you can do to improve the situation. Shifting from blame to action empowers you to take control and find solutions.

3. Be Accountable

Hold yourself accountable for your commitments and promises. If you say you're going to do something, follow through. If you make a mistake, own up to it and make amends. Accountability builds trust and integrity.

4. Make Conscious Choices

Be intentional with your decisions. Consider how your choices align with your goals and values and consider their potential consequences. Making conscious choices helps you create the life you want rather than drifting aimlessly.

5. Learn from Mistakes

Everyone makes mistakes, but taking responsibility means using those mistakes as learning opportunities. Reflect on what went wrong and how you can do better next time. This approach turns failures into stepping stones toward success.

BHAGAT SINGH'S COURAGE

Bhagat Singh was born in 1907 in Punjab, India, during British colonial rule. From a young age, he was deeply affected by the injustices and oppression he witnessed. Inspired by the nationalist movements and the desire for freedom, he dedicated his life to fighting for India's independence.

At just 23 years old, Bhagat Singh understood that achieving freedom required bold and decisive actions. He took it upon himself to stand against the British rule, knowing the risks involved. He believed that staying silent or passive in the face of injustice was equivalent to supporting it.

In 1929, he and his associates carried out a dramatic protest by throwing harmless bombs in the Central Legislative Assembly, shouting slogans of revolution, and willingly surrendering to the authorities. Their intent was not to harm but to make their voices heard and to awaken the masses to the need for action. Bhagat Singh was arrested and faced trial for his actions. Throughout the trial, he remained steadfast and unapologetic, using the courtroom to advocate for India's freedom and explain the motives behind his actions.

He accepted full responsibility, knowing that it would likely lead to his execution. Despite immense pressure, he refused to seek mercy or compromise his principles. His courage and willingness to accept the consequences of his actions inspired countless others to join the struggle for independence.

Bhagat Singh was executed in 1931, but his legacy lived on. His act of taking responsibility and standing up against oppression became a powerful symbol of resistance and inspired a generation of freedom fighters. His story teaches us that taking responsibility can lead to profound and lasting change, even in great danger.

This story powerfully reminds us of what taking responsibility can achieve. While most of us won't face challenges on such a grand scale, the principle remains the same: when we take responsibility for our lives, we unlock our potential to effect meaningful change.

Whether improving your relationships, advancing in your career, or contributing to your community, embracing responsibility empowers you to create your desired life. It all starts with a simple decision to own your actions and choices fully. It's about making conscious choices, learning from your experiences, and striving to be your best version. It's not always easy, but the rewards are immeasurable.

CHAPTER TWO

Your Inner Guide: Learning to Rely on Yourself in a Noisy World

I want you to imagine a situation where you've got a big decision to make—something that could really impact your life. Maybe it's about your career, your relationships, or a personal project you've been dreaming about. You start weighing your options, but instead of trusting your judgment, you immediately seek advice from everyone around you. You ask your friends, family, and maybe even your coworkers because you're afraid of making the wrong choice.

Now, there's nothing wrong with asking for advice, but when you rely on others to make decisions for you, you're giving away your power. You're saying, "I don't trust myself to handle this." And that's where self-reliance comes in.

Self-reliance is about trusting yourself—your instincts,

your abilities, your judgment. It's about knowing that you can handle it no matter what comes your way. And when you cultivate self-reliance, you build confidence, independence, and a deeper sense of personal power.

Understanding Self-Reliance

Self-reliance isn't just about doing everything on your own or refusing help when you need it. It's about having the confidence to know that you can take care of yourself, make your own decisions, and trust that you can handle whatever comes your way.

When you're self-reliant, you believe in your ability to think for yourself. You don't wait for someone else to tell you what to do or how to do it. Instead, you take the initiative and trust your judgment.

But self-reliance goes beyond just decision-making. It's also about taking responsibility for your happiness, success, and well-being. It's about understanding that you are the architect of your own life and have the power to shape your future.

Why Self-Reliance Matters

So, why is self-reliance so important? Because it's the foundation of independence and empowerment. Without self-reliance, you're constantly looking to others for approval, guidance, and direction. You become dependent on external factors to feel secure and confident.

When you rely too much on others, you may doubt your abilities. You might think, "What if I make the wrong choice?" or "What if I can't handle this alone?" This thinking keeps you stuck, afraid to take risks or make changes. It makes you feel small and powerless.

On the other hand, when you cultivate self-reliance, you build a strong sense of self. You know that, even if you make mistakes, you can learn from them and move forward. You trust yourself to handle whatever challenges come your way. This confidence spills over into every aspect of your life, making you more resilient, adaptable, and proactive.

The Shift from Dependence to Self-Reliance

I used to be someone who relied heavily on others for validation. I'd second-guess my decisions and constantly seek reassurance from friends and family. I feared making mistakes and felt I needed someone else to guide me.

But over time, I realised that this way of thinking was holding me back. I wasn't growing because I wasn't trusting myself to take risks and make decisions. I lived in constant doubt and fear, always wondering if I was doing the right thing.

The turning point came when I started practising self-reliance. I decided to trust my instincts, even if they went against the advice of others. I began making decisions based on what felt right for me, rather than what others thought I should do.

At first, it was uncomfortable. I worried about making mistakes or disappointing people. But as I continued to trust myself, I noticed something amazing happening—I started to feel more confident and empowered. I was no longer waiting for someone else to give me permission to live my life. I was taking control, and it felt liberating.

How to Build Self-Reliance

Building self-reliance is a process, and it requires practice and patience. Here are some practical steps you can take to start developing self-reliance in your daily life:

1. Start Small

Self-reliance doesn't have to start with big, life-changing decisions. You can begin by trusting yourself with smaller tasks and choices. For example, if you're used to asking for opinions on what to wear or eat, try making those decisions yourself. Gradually, as you build confidence in these small areas, you'll find it easier to trust yourself with bigger decisions.

2. Embrace Mistakes

One of people's biggest fears about being self-reliant is the fear of making mistakes. But mistakes are a natural part of life and essential for growth. Instead of fearing mistakes, embrace them as learning opportunities. When you make a mistake, please don't dwell on it. Instead, ask yourself, "What can I learn from this?" and move forward with that knowledge.

3. Trust Your Instincts

Your instincts are powerful guides. When faced with a decision, take a moment to listen to your gut feeling. What is it telling you? Often, your instincts will point you in the right direction. Trusting your instincts is a key component of self-reliance, and it helps you build confidence in your ability to make good decisions.

4. Take Initiative

Self-reliance means taking charge of your life rather than waiting for others to lead the way. Start taking the initiative in your daily life. If there's something you want to achieve, don't wait for someone else to push you—take the first step yourself. Whether starting a new project, learning a new skill, or pursuing a personal goal, taking the initiative empowers you to create the life you want.

5. Rely on Yourself First

When you encounter a problem, challenge yourself to find a solution before seeking help. This doesn't mean you should never ask for help—there's value in collaboration and support—but you should give yourself the chance to solve the problem first. The more you rely on yourself, the more confident you'll become in your abilities.

6. Set Personal Boundaries

Self-reliance also involves setting boundaries with others. This means knowing when to say no, when to stand up for yourself, and when to prioritise your own needs. By setting boundaries, you protect your energy and ensure that you're not relying on others to fulfil your needs or make you happy.

ANJU BALA'S JOURNEY TO SELF RELIANCE

Anju Bala, a woman from a small village in Haryana, India, who transformed her life by embracing self-reliance. Anju Bala grew up in a traditional village where women were often expected to stay home and not pursue careers. Her husband worked as an AC repairman while Anju cared for the household. But Anju had dreams of her own. She wanted to contribute financially and build something of her own, but she faced many obstacles—cultural norms, lack of resources, and limited opportunities.

Despite these challenges, Anju didn't give up on her dreams. She knew that to create a better life for herself and her family, she would have to rely on her abilities and take initiative.

Anju's journey toward self-reliance began when she participated in the DISHA project, a program designed to empower women by providing them with the skills and confidence to start their own businesses. Through this project, Anju learned about tailoring and beauty parlour management—skills she could use to start her own business. But learning the skills was just the beginning. Anju had to overcome the doubts of those around her, including her husband, who was initially unsupportive of her ambitions. Instead of waiting for others to validate her dreams, Anju trusted herself and moved forward.

She started a small tailoring business from home, and with the money she earned, she saved up to open a beauty parlour in her village. Anju's determination and self-reliance paid off, and she became a role model for other women in her community.

Anju's story is a powerful example of how self-reliance can transform your life. By trusting herself and taking initiative, she overcame her environment's limitations and created a successful business. She didn't wait for permission or approval—she trusted her instincts and took control of her destiny.

Anju's success also had a ripple effect in her community. Inspired by her journey, other women began to pursue their own dreams and embrace self-reliance. Anju's story shows that when you take responsibility for your life and trust yourself, you not only change your own life but also inspire others to do the same.

Trust Yourself and Take Control
Self-reliance is about more than just doing things on your own—it's about believing in your ability to shape your life and make the right decisions. It's about trusting yourself to handle whatever comes your way and knowing that you have the power to create the future you want.

It's something you build over time through practice and experience. Start small, embrace your mistakes, and trust your instincts. The more you rely on yourself, the more confident and empowered you'll become.

CHAPTER THREE

No More Excuses: How Owning Your Actions Unlocks Freedom

Have you ever found yourself in a situation where something went wrong, and your first instinct was to find someone or something to blame? Maybe you missed a deadline and blamed it on your busy schedule, or you didn't achieve a goal and blamed it on circumstances beyond your control. It's a natural reaction, and we've all done it at some point. But here's the truth: when we blame others or external factors, we're avoiding the one thing that could actually help us grow—accountability.

Accountability is about owning your actions, your decisions, and their outcomes. It's about recognising that you are responsible for what happens in your life, both the successes and the failures. When you hold yourself accountable, you take control. You stop waiting for others to fix things for you and start making changes yourself.

Let's explore what I mean by accountability and how it's

more than just taking the blame when something goes wrong. At its core, accountability is about taking ownership of your entire life. It's about recognizing that you have a role in everything that happens to you—both the good and the bad. This might sound heavy, but it's incredibly empowering.

Let me share a personal example to illustrate this. In one of the organizations where I used to work, we conducted a large hiring drive. We had ambitious targets to meet and a clear plan in place. Despite putting in a lot of effort—coordinating with teams, scheduling interviews, and reaching out to numerous candidates—we fell short of filling the number of vacancies we aimed for.

When the final number came in, I felt frustrated. My first instinct was to blame the circumstances—the limited talent pool, candidates dropping out at the last minute, or even team members who didn't seem to share the same urgency. But deep down, I realized that shifting blame wouldn't change the outcome. I had to take responsibility for the situation and look for ways to improve our approach moving forward.

But then I took a step back and thought about accountability. Instead of focusing on what everyone else had done or what had gone wrong around me, I asked myself, "What was my role in this? What could I have done differently?" It wasn't an easy question because it meant admitting that I wasn't just a victim of bad circumstances—I was a participant in the outcome.

I realised that I could have managed my time better while

the deadlines were tight. While the resources were limited, I could have been more creative in finding solutions. While some team members didn't meet my expectations, I could have communicated more clearly and offered better support to help them succeed. Acknowledging these things didn't mean I was to blame for everything that went wrong, but it did mean that I had power over certain aspects of the project and could have made different choices.

This is what accountability is all about. It's about understanding that you have a role in your successes and your failures. When you're accountable, you don't just say, "This didn't work because of X, Y, and Z." Instead, you say, "Here's what I did, here's what I could have done better, and here's what I'll do next time to improve." This mindset shifts your focus from what's outside of your control to what's within your control. And that's where real change happens.

By taking ownership of my role in that project, I learned valuable lessons that I applied to future projects. I became more proactive in managing my time, more resourceful in finding solutions, and more effective in leading my team. The next project I worked on was a success, and it was because I took the lessons from that earlier failure and used them to make better choices.

When you practice accountability in this way, you stop feeling like life is happening to you, and you start feeling like you're the one making things happen. You're no longer at the mercy of external factors—you're in control. This doesn't mean that you won't face challenges or that everything will always go your way, but it does mean that

you'll approach each situation with a mindset that's focused on growth and improvement.

Another example of accountability in action comes from a friend who struggles to maintain a healthy lifestyle. She would start a new diet or exercise routine for years, only to give up after a few weeks. She'd blame her busy schedule, lack of motivation, or even her friends for not supporting her. But then she realised nothing would change if she kept blaming everything around her.

So, she decided to take accountability for her health. She acknowledged that while her schedule was busy, she had the power to make time for what was important to her. She recognised that while motivation comes and goes, she could build discipline by committing to and sticking to her goals, even when she didn't like it. She also understood that while it's great to have support, her health was ultimately her responsibility.

She started making small, consistent changes by taking ownership of her health. She began scheduling her workouts like important meetings that she couldn't cancel. She planned her meals to avoid last-minute unhealthy choices. She also held herself accountable by tracking her progress and celebrating her small wins.

The result?

She achieved her health goals and gained more profound confidence and control over her life. She stopped relying on external factors to dictate her success and started relying on herself. And that's the power of accountability.

When you take accountability, you're not just admitting when you're wrong. You're taking control of your life. You're saying, "I have the power to make different choices, and I'm committed to making better ones." This mindset is transformative because it empowers you to create the life you want rather than being a passive observer of what happens around you.

So the next time you find yourself in a situation where things didn't go as planned, resist the urge to blame someone or something else. Instead, ask yourself, "What was my role in this? What can I do differently next time?" This simple shift in perspective can make a world of difference. It puts you in the driver's seat of your life, where you belong.

Why Accountability Matters?

Why is accountability so crucial? It's the foundation of trust, growth, and personal integrity.

1. Building Trust
When you hold yourself accountable, others trust you more. Accountability shows you're reliable and honest in personal relationships or professional life. People know that you'll own up to your mistakes and work to correct them rather than shifting the blame. This builds more substantial, more trusting relationships.

2. Personal Growth
Accountability is essential for personal growth. When you take responsibility for your actions, you can learn from

your mistakes. Instead of seeing failures as setbacks, you see them as improvement opportunities. This mindset helps you grow and develop in ways you never could if you constantly made excuses.

3. Integrity

Owning your actions is a key component of integrity. When you're accountable, you align your actions with your values. You do what you say you'll do and follow through on your commitments. This consistency between your words and actions builds integrity and earns you respect from others.

How to Start Practicing Accountability

If you want to take control of your life, accountability is key. Here are some practical steps to help you start practising accountability in your daily life:

1. Own Your Mistakes

The first step to accountability is admitting when you're wrong. When something goes wrong, resist blaming others or making excuses. Instead, ask yourself, "What role did I play in this?" and "What can I do to make it right?" Owning your mistakes is not about self-blame but about recognising where you can improve.

2. Reflect on Your Actions

Accountability requires self-reflection. Take time to regularly reflect on your actions, decisions, and their outcomes. Ask yourself, "Did I act in alignment with my values?" and "What could I have done better?" This practice helps you stay aware of your behaviour and encourages continuous improvement.

3. Set Clear Goals and Expectations

To hold yourself accountable, you need to know what you're aiming for. Set clear, specific goals for yourself in your personal and professional life. Then, set expectations for how you will achieve those goals. A clear roadmap allows you to measure your progress and hold yourself accountable for staying on track.

4. Follow Through on Commitments

When you commit—whether to yourself or others—honour it. If you say you're going to do something, do it. Following through on your commitments builds trust and reinforces your sense of accountability.

5. Seek Feedback

One of the best ways to practice accountability is to seek feedback from others. Ask people you trust for their honest opinions about your actions and behaviour. This can provide valuable insights and help you see areas where you might need to improve. Remember, feedback is not a criticism—it's an opportunity to grow.

DRONACHARYA'S COMPLEX ACCOUNTABILITY

To really grasp the incredible power and depth of accountability, let's dive into the story of Dronacharya, a legendary figure from the Mahabharata. His journey beautifully illustrates the unique challenges and responsibilities that accompany the essence of being accountable.

Dronacharya was the royal guru of the Kauravas and Pandavas, the two factions in the Mahabharata. He was a master of advanced military arts and was deeply respected by his students. However, his role as a teacher came with immense responsibilities and ethical dilemmas.

One of the most significant challenges Dronacharya faced was his relationship with Ekalavya, a young tribal boy who admired him deeply. Ekalavya, despite not being formally trained by Dronacharya, became an exceptional archer by practising in front of a clay statue of the guru. When Dronacharya discovered this, he was faced with a moral dilemma. He had promised Arjuna, his favourite student, that he would make him the greatest archer. But Ekalavya's skill posed a threat to this promise.

In a decision that has been debated for centuries, Dronacharya asked Ekalavya for his thumb as guru dakshina (teacher's fee), knowing that this would limit Ekalavya's ability to surpass Arjuna. Ekalavya, out of deep respect and devotion, complied without hesitation.

This decision made by Dronacharya shines a light on the intricate nature of accountability. On one side, he had a commitment to Arjuna and the promise he made to him. On the other side, he also had a responsibility to ensure fair treatment for all his students. While his decision aimed to protect Arjuna's standing, it brings up important discussions about fairness, ethics, and the real essence of being a teacher.

Dronacharya's story teaches us that accountability isn't always clear-cut. Sometimes, being accountable means making difficult choices, and those choices can have far-reaching consequences. Dronacharya was accountable for the decisions he made, and those decisions shaped the course of the Mahabharata.

This story reminds us that accountability is not just about taking responsibility for the good things in life but also for the difficult decisions and their outcomes. It's about being willing to face the consequences of your actions, even when they are complex and challenging.

Accountability is a powerful tool for gaining control of one's life. When one takes ownership of one's actions and their outcomes, one empowers oneself to create wonderful, positive change. One can stop waiting for others to improve and start making better choices on one's own journey.

Accountability is like a journey we embark on together; it's not just about a single moment in time. It requires our ongoing self-reflection, honesty, and dedication to keep growing and improving. The journey brings wonderful rewards, such as building greater trust, experiencing personal growth, and embracing a deeper sense of integrity.

CHAPTER FOUR

The Growth Mindset: Turning Roadblocks into Stepping Stones

"I've been in this position for years, and no matter what I do, I can't seem to move forward." If you've ever felt like this, you're not alone. We all face obstacles in life that seem impossible—whether in our careers, personal lives, or even within ourselves. These obstacles can make us feel stuck, frustrated, and even hopeless. But here's the truth: obstacles are a natural part of life. Everyone faces them, but what sets successful people apart is their ability to overcome them.

Understanding Obstacles
Before we dive into how to overcome obstacles, let's first understand what they are. Obstacles are anything that stands in the way of your progress. They can be external, like financial difficulties, lack of resources, or unsupportive environments. They can also be internal, like fear, self-doubt, or limiting beliefs. Sometimes, the biggest barriers are the ones we create in our own minds.

It's easy to see obstacles as roadblocks that stop us from reaching our goals. But in reality, obstacles are opportunities in disguise. They challenge us to grow, to become more resilient, and to find new ways to achieve our goals. When you learn to see obstacles this way, they become less intimidating and more manageable.

Shifting Your Mindset
The first step in overcoming obstacles is to shift your mindset. If you approach challenges with a negative or defeatist attitude, they'll seem even more daunting. But if you see them as opportunities to learn and grow, you'll be more motivated to tackle them head-on.

I want you to really think about a time when you faced a significant challenge. Maybe it was something at work, like a project that seemed impossible to complete. Or perhaps it was a personal setback—something that shook your confidence and made you question whether you could get through it. It could even be a situation that pushed you far out of your comfort zone, forcing you to deal with uncertainty, fear, or even failure.

As you reflect on that challenge, ask yourself: How did you approach it? Did you spend most of your time and energy focusing on the problem, thinking about how difficult, unfair, or overwhelming it was? Or did you start looking for solutions, no matter how small they might have seemed at the time? This is a crucial distinction because how you respond to challenges can keep you stuck or help you grow.

When you're faced with a difficult situation, it's natural

to feel fear and doubt. These emotions are part of being human. But here's the thing: what you do with those emotions makes all the difference. If you let fear and doubt take over, they can paralyze you. You might find yourself stuck in a cycle of overthinking, worrying, and feeling helpless. It's like standing at the base of a mountain, staring up at how high and steep it is, and feeling too overwhelmed to take the first step.

I've been there. I know what it's like to feel overwhelmed by a challenge, to focus so much on the problem size that you forget even to consider possible solutions. But I've also learned that the key to overcoming these obstacles is to shift your focus. Instead of fixating on the problem, start looking for ways to move forward—even if it's just one small step at a time.

There was a time when I was assigned a project at work that seemed completely beyond my capabilities. The scope was huge, the deadline was tight, and the expectations were sky-high. My first reaction was to focus on everything that could go wrong. I thought about how little time I had, how much there was to do, and how everyone would count on me to deliver. The more I thought about it, the more anxious I became. I started doubting myself—what if I failed? What if I let everyone down?

For a while, I let those fears consume me. I spent days worrying about the project, thinking about why it might not work out. I was so focused on the problem that I couldn't see any way forward. But then, something shifted. I realised I wouldn't get anywhere if I stayed in this mindset. I was going to stay stuck in my fear and doubt.

So, I made a conscious decision to change my approach. Instead of focusing on everything that could go wrong, I started asking myself, "What can I do to make this work?" I broke the project down into smaller tasks, and I focused on completing one thing at a time. I asked for help when I needed it, and I didn't let my pride stop me from seeking advice from others who had more experience. Each small step I took helped build my confidence, and slowly, I began to see progress.

By shifting my focus from the problem to the solution, I was able to push through the fear and doubt. The project ended up being a success, but more importantly, I learned that I could handle challenges that initially seemed impossible. That experience taught me that no matter how overwhelming a situation might seem, there's always a way forward—you must be willing to look for it.

So, think back to your challenge.
Did you focus on the problem or start looking for solutions?
Did you let fear and doubt hold you back, or did you push through and find a way forward?

If you find yourself stuck, focusing on the problem and letting fear take over, don't be too hard on yourself. It happens to all of us. But use this as an opportunity to reflect and grow. Next time you face a challenge, try to shift your mindset. Focus on what you can do, not on what might go wrong. Start taking small steps, even if they seem insignificant at first. Each step will bring you closer to overcoming the obstacle, and with each step, you'll build the confidence to keep going.

I won't pretend that this is always easy. There will be times when the obstacles you face seem overwhelming, when the fear and doubt are strong, and when the path forward isn't clear. But it's in those moments that you have the opportunity to prove to yourself just how resilient and resourceful you can be. And every time you do, you'll come out stronger, more confident, and more prepared for whatever life throws.

So, the next time you face a challenge, remember this: focus on solutions, not problems. Push through the fear and doubt. Take one small step at a time. Know that you have the strength and determination to overcome any obstacle.

When you shift your mindset from "I can't" to "How can I?" you open yourself up to possibilities. You start to see obstacles not as barriers but as puzzles to be solved. This mindset shift is crucial because it empowers you to act rather than feel paralysed by fear or frustration.

Common Obstacles and How to Overcome Them
Let's look at some common obstacles many people face and explore strategies for overcoming them.

1. Fear of Failure
Fear of failure is one of the most common obstacles people face. It can stop you from pursuing your goals, taking risks, or trying something new. The fear of failing can be so overwhelming that it paralyses you, keeping you stuck in your comfort zone.

The key to overcoming the fear of failure is to redefine what failure means to you. Instead of seeing failure as something negative, start seeing it as a learning opportunity. Every time you fail, you gain valuable insights that can help you improve and grow. Embrace failure as a natural part of the learning process. Remember, the only real failure is not trying at all.

2. Lack of Resources

Another common obstacle is a lack of resources, such as time, money, or support. It's easy to feel like you can't move forward because you lack what you need to succeed.

While it's true that resources are important, they're not the only factor in achieving success. Focus on what you do have and how you can leverage it to your advantage. Be resourceful and creative in finding solutions. Sometimes, the lack of resources forces you to think outside the box and come up with innovative ideas that you wouldn't have considered otherwise.

3. Self-Doubt

Self-doubt is a powerful internal obstacle that can hold you back from reaching your full potential. It's that nagging voice in your head that tells you you're not good enough, that you don't have what it takes, or that you're going to fail.

Overcoming self-doubt requires building confidence in yourself and your abilities. Start by challenging those negative thoughts. Ask yourself, "Is this really true, or am I just letting fear take over?" Focus on your strengths and successes, and remind yourself of the times when you overcame challenges. Surround yourself with supportive people who believe in you and can help you see your potential.

4. Procrastination
Procrastination is another common obstacle that can prevent progress. It's easy to put off tasks, especially when they seem overwhelming or you're unsure where to start.

The best way to overcome procrastination is to break tasks down into smaller, more manageable steps. Set clear goals and deadlines for yourself, and take action, even if it's just a small step. The key is to build momentum. Once you start making progress, it becomes easier to keep going.

THE JOURNEY OF BHAICHUNG BHUTIA: OVERCOMING THE ODDS

Bhaichung Bhutia's journey is a powerful example of how determination, resilience, and a positive mindset can help you overcome obstacles and achieve your dreams.

Bhaichung Bhutia was born in a small village in Sikkim, India. He faced numerous challenges as a child, including limited access to proper training facilities and a lack of resources. However, Bhaichung was passionate about football and determined to succeed, no matter the obstacles.

Despite his humble beginnings, Bhaichung never let his circumstances define him. He practised tirelessly, often using makeshift equipment and playing on rough terrain. His love for the game and unwavering determination kept him going, even when the odds were stacked against him.

As Bhaichung's skills improved, he began to attract attention. But his journey to the top was not without setbacks. He faced tough competition from more experienced players, dealt with injuries, and had moments of self-doubt. But each time he encountered an obstacle, Bhaichung saw it as an opportunity to learn and grow.

He pushed himself to work harder, to refine his skills, and to prove to himself and others that he had what it took to succeed. His perseverance paid off when he was selected to play for some of India's top football clubs, including East Bengal and Mohun Bagan. His talent and determination eventually earned him a contract with Bury FC in England, making him the first Indian player to play professional football in Europe.

Bhaichung Bhutia's story is not just about personal success; it's about overcoming the odds and inspiring others to do the same. His journey shows that no matter where you start or the obstacles you face, you can achieve greatness if you're willing to work hard, stay focused, and never give up.

Bhaichung's legacy continues to inspire young athletes across India and beyond. He has shown that anything is possible with determination, resilience, and a positive mindset.

Obstacles are inevitable, but they don't have to stop you from reaching your goals. They can be the very thing that pushes you to grow, to think creatively, and to become stronger.

Overcoming obstacles starts with a mindset shift. Instead of seeing challenges as roadblocks, start seeing them as opportunities to learn and grow. Embrace the lessons they offer and use them to fuel your determination.

CHAPTER FIVE

Stronger Together: How Responsibility Transforms Relationships

"I don't understand why my relationships always seem to hit a wall. No matter what I do, things don't seem to work out."

If you've ever had these thoughts, you're not alone. Relationships can be challenging with friends, family, colleagues, or a partner. They require constant effort, communication, and understanding. But there's one key element that can make a world of difference: responsibility.

Taking responsibility in your relationships means owning your actions, words, and emotions. It means recognising your impact on others and being accountable for how you contribute to the relationship. When you embrace responsibility, you stop blaming others for what goes wrong and focus on what you can do to improve the connection. This mindset shift can lead to deeper, more fulfilling relationships that stand the test of time.

Understanding Responsibility in Relationships

At its core, responsibility in relationships is about ownership—owning your actions, words, and feelings and their impact on others. It's about recognising that you have a role in the dynamics of the relationship and that your behaviour contributes to the overall health of that connection.

When things go wrong in a relationship, it's easy to point fingers and blame the other person. "If only they would change, things would be better." But this approach only creates distance and resentment. It keeps you in a cycle of frustration because you're waiting for someone else to fix the problem.

But what if, instead of focusing on what the other person is doing wrong, you concentrate on what you can do differently? What if you took responsibility for your part in the relationship, even if it's just a small part? This shift in perspective can transform the way you interact with others. It empowers you to take action, to make changes, and to improve the relationship from your side. And often, when you change your approach, the other person responds in kind, leading to a healthier, more positive dynamic.

Let's explore some common challenges people face in relationships and how taking responsibility can help address them.

1. Communication Breakdowns

One of the most common issues in relationships is communication breakdowns. Misunderstandings, assumptions, and lack of clear communication can lead to conflicts and hurt feelings. When communication breaks down, it's easy to blame the other person for not listening or not understanding you.

Let me share the story of Anita and Rahul, a working couple from Mumbai, to illustrate the power of taking responsibility for communication in relationships. Both have demanding careers—Anita is a marketing manager for an FMCG company, and Rahul is an IT consultant. Their long work hours, deadlines, and personal commitments often left them exhausted. Over time, they started experiencing tension in their relationship.

Anita would get frustrated when Rahul didn't help with household chores, while Rahul felt unappreciated and thought Anita didn't understand the pressures of his job. Small misunderstandings grew into arguments, and both of them assumed the other should just know what they were feeling.

One evening, after a particularly tense argument, they realized things had to change. Instead of continuing to blame each other, they decided to take responsibility for their communication. They agreed to have open, honest conversations about their needs and expectations. Anita expressed how overwhelmed she felt managing work and home duties, while Rahul shared how he sometimes felt disconnected after long, stressful days.

They set a simple rule: every evening, they would spend 20 minutes discussing their day without distractions. Anita clearly expressed her need for help, and Rahul actively listened instead of planning his response while she spoke. Likewise, Rahul communicated his feelings of needing time to unwind after work, and Anita acknowledged this. They also began asking each other, "How can I support you today?"

Taking responsibility for communication transformed their relationship. By proactively expressing their needs and truly listening to each other, they deepened their understanding and strengthened their bond. Misunderstandings became rare, and mutual respect flourished.

2. Unrealistic Expectations
Another common challenge in relationships is having unrealistic expectations of the other person. Expecting your partner, friend, or family member to fulfil all your needs, always understand you, or never make mistakes can lead to disappointment and resentment when these expectations aren't met. This can create a rift in the relationship and hinder effective communication.

Taking responsibility means recognising that no one person can meet all your needs or be perfect all the time. It means managing your expectations and understanding that the other person is human, with their own flaws and limitations. Instead of placing the burden of your happiness or fulfilment on someone else, take responsibility for meeting your own needs. This doesn't mean you shouldn't expect anything from your relationships, but it does mean being realistic and fair in your expectations. When you take responsibility for your own happiness, you reduce the pressure on the other person, leading to a healthier and more balanced relationship. It's a relief to know that you don't have to carry the weight of unrealistic expectations.

3. Avoiding Conflict

Many people struggle to avoid conflict in their relationships. They might fear that addressing an issue will lead to an argument or that the other person will react negatively. As a result, they avoid difficult conversations, allowing problems to fester and grow over time. However, it's important to remember that addressing conflict can lead to growth and a deeper understanding of relationships.

Taking responsibility in conflict situations means being willing to address issues head-on, rather than avoiding them. It means recognising that conflict, when handled properly, can lead to growth and a deeper understanding of each other. Instead of sweeping issues under the rug, please take responsibility for bringing them to light in a respectful and constructive manner. This doesn't mean being confrontational but being honest and open about your feelings and concerns. This approach allows you to resolve conflicts before they become more significant problems and build a stronger foundation for the relationship.

4. Lack of Appreciation

Another common issue in relationships is a lack of appreciation. Over time, it's easy to take the other person for granted, assuming they know how much you care without expressing it. This can lead to feelings of neglect and resentment.

Taking responsibility for showing appreciation means making an effort to acknowledge and express gratitude for the other person's contributions to the relationship. Whether it's a small gesture or a significant effort, taking the time to say "thank you" or to show your appreciation in other ways can make a big difference. It reinforces your value on the relationship and helps the other person feel valued and respected.

Now that we've explored some common challenges and how responsibility can help let's look at practical steps you can take to enhance your relationships through responsibility.

1. Reflect on Your Role
The first step in taking responsibility is reflecting on your role in the relationship. Ask yourself, "How am I contributing to the dynamics of this relationship?" Be honest with yourself about your actions, words, and attitudes. Consider how you can make positive changes to improve the relationship.

2. Communicate Openly and Honestly
Good communication is the foundation of any healthy relationship. Take responsibility for how you communicate with others. Be clear, honest, and respectful in your interactions. Try to listen actively and understand the other person's perspective. When issues arise, address them directly rather than avoiding them.

3. Manage Your Expectations
Take responsibility for managing your expectations of

others. Recognize that no one is perfect and that everyone has limitations. Be realistic in what you expect from the relationship and avoid placing undue pressure on the other person to meet all your needs.

4. Show Appreciation

Try to express your appreciation for the other person regularly. Whether it's through words, actions, or gestures, let them know that you value their presence in your life. Taking responsibility for showing appreciation can strengthen your bond and build a more positive relationship.

5. Address Conflicts Constructively

When conflicts arise, take responsibility for addressing them constructively. Approach the situation with a mindset of resolution rather than blame. Be willing to have difficult conversations and work through issues together. This approach can lead to deeper understanding and a stronger relationship.

AMITABH AND JAYA BACHCHAN: A PARTNERSHIP BUILT ON RESPONSIBILITY

To truly understand the power of responsibility in relationships, let's look at the story of Amitabh and Jaya Bachchan, one of Bollywood's most iconic couples. Their journey together shows how mutual respect, communication, and shared responsibility can create a lasting and fulfilling partnership.

Amitabh and Jaya Bachchan first met in the early 1970s on the set of the film Guddi. Their connection was immediate, and they quickly developed a deep respect for each other's talent, intellect, and character. This mutual respect became the foundation of their relationship.

They have faced numerous challenges throughout their marriage, from the pressures of fame and public scrutiny to personal and professional setbacks. However, they have taken responsibility for nurturing their relationship and ensuring it remains strong and supportive.

One key element of Amitabh and Jaya's relationship is their ability to navigate life's challenges together. They have always approached their partnership as a team, sharing responsibility for their family, careers, and personal growth.

For example, when Amitabh faced a near-fatal accident on the set of "Coolie" in 1982, Jaya stood by his side, providing unwavering support throughout his recovery. She managed their home and ensured that their family remained strong during this difficult time. Her dedication and strength were instrumental in Amitabh's recovery and keeping their family united.

Communication has always been a priority for Amitabh and Jaya. They understand that open and honest communication is essential for maintaining a healthy relationship. Whether discussing their work, their children, or their personal feelings, they have always made it a point to keep the lines of communication open. This commitment to communication has helped them navigate the ups and downs of life together, ensuring that misunderstandings are addressed and that they remain connected and in tune with each other's needs.

Amitabh and Jaya Bachchan's relationship is a powerful example of how taking responsibility in a relationship can lead to lasting success. Their mutual respect, shared responsibilities, and commitment to communication have allowed them to build a partnership that has stood the test of time.

Their story reminds us that relationships require effort, understanding, and a willingness to take responsibility for our actions. We create a strong foundation for weathering storms when we embrace responsibility in our relationships.

Strengthening Your Relationships Through Responsibility

Relationships are among the most essential aspects of life, but they can also be among the most challenging. By taking responsibility for your actions, words, and emotions, you can enhance your relationships and build stronger, more fulfilling connections with the people you care about.

Amitabh and Jaya Bachchan's story is an inspiring example of how mutual respect, communication, and shared responsibility can create a lasting and successful partnership. Their journey together reminds us that when we take responsibility for our relationships, we improve our lives and positively impact those around us.

I encourage you to reflect on your relationships and consider how you can take responsibility for enhancing them. Remember that it's not about blaming yourself or others but about owning your role in the relationship and making positive changes.

CHAPTER SIX

Career on Purpose: Taking Charge of Your Professional Journey

"I've been in the same job for years and don't see any growth. It feels like I'm stuck, no matter how hard I work."

If you've ever had this thought, you're not alone. Many people sometimes feel trapped in their careers, wondering why their hard work isn't translating into progress. The truth is, thriving in your career isn't just about putting in long hours or doing your job well. It's about taking professional responsibility—owning your actions, decisions, and growth within your career.

Professional responsibility means more than showing up to work and completing tasks. It's about actively managing your career, making intentional decisions, and being accountable for your successes and failures. When you take responsibility for your professional life, you empower yourself to create the career you want rather than just waiting for opportunities to come to you.

Professional responsibility involves a combination of self-accountability, proactive decision-making, and a commitment to continuous improvement. It's about recognising that your career is in your hands—you can shape it through the choices you make, the actions you take, and the mindset you cultivate.

You don't just do the bare minimum when you take professional responsibility. You actively seek ways to improve, contribute, and grow within your role. You take ownership of your mistakes and successes and view challenges as opportunities to learn and develop.

So why is professional responsibility so important? Because it's the foundation of a successful and fulfilling career.

1. It Builds Trust and Credibility
When you consistently take responsibility for your work, others trust you more. Your colleagues and supervisors know they can rely on you to deliver on your commitments, to admit when you've made a mistake, and to take the necessary steps to fix it. This trust is crucial for building strong professional relationships and advancing your career.

2. It Encourages Growth and Development
Taking responsibility for your career means always looking for ways to improve. You don't wait for someone else to push you—you seek opportunities for learning and growth. This proactive approach helps you develop new skills, gain more experience, and position yourself for more significant opportunities.

3. It Empowers You to Shape Your Career
When you take responsibility for your career, you stop waiting for things to happen and start making them happen. You take control of your professional trajectory, making intentional decisions about where you want to go and how you will get there. This empowerment is key to creating a career that aligns with your goals and aspirations.

The Shift from Passive to Proactive
One of the biggest shifts that comes with taking professional responsibility is moving from a passive to a proactive mindset. Instead of waiting for opportunities to come to you, you create them. Instead of reacting to situations, you plan and make decisions that align with your long-term goals.

Early in my career as an HR professional, I firmly believed that hard work alone would lead to success. I dedicated myself to my tasks—processing payroll on time, managing employee relations, and ensuring compliance with company policies. I thought that if I kept my head down, performed diligently, and met deadlines, my efforts would naturally be noticed and rewarded. I expected my managers to see the value I brought and to hand me opportunities for growth and advancement.

But as time passed, nothing changed. I was meeting expectations, but the recognition I hoped for never came. My career seemed stagnant, and the promotions or new challenges I longed for remained out of reach. I grew frustrated, questioning why my dedication wasn't translating into progress. It took a moment of self-reflection to understand the problem: I wasn't taking responsibility for my career growth while I was putting in the work. I waited for opportunities to be handed to me instead of actively seeking them out.

I realized I needed to shift from a passive to a proactive mindset, so I took deliberate steps to change my approach. I began setting clear career goals and communicating them with my manager during performance reviews. Instead of waiting for projects to come my way, I volunteered for new initiatives, particularly those that stretched my abilities and visibility within the organization. For instance, I proposed and led a project to streamline the onboarding process, improving efficiency and demonstrating my ability to take initiative and drive change.

I also sought out mentorship and feedback. I approached senior leaders and asked for their advice on how to grow in my role. Their guidance helped me identify areas for improvement, such as developing stronger communication skills and learning more about HR analytics. With this feedback, I took courses, attended workshops, and applied what I learned in my daily work.

As I took responsibility for my professional growth, things began to change. My proactive attitude was noticed, and soon, opportunities that once seemed out of reach started coming my way. I was trusted with more strategic projects; eventually, these efforts led to promotions and greater responsibilities.

This shift taught me a valuable lesson: waiting for recognition isn't a strategy for success. Taking responsibility for your career means actively communicating your aspirations, seeking opportunities, and consistently demonstrating your value. In HR—and in any field—your growth is in your hands. By taking charge of your path, you empower yourself to achieve the success you envision.

When you take this proactive approach, you're no longer at the mercy of external circumstances. You become the driver of your career, making decisions that align with your goals and values. This mindset shift is empowering and opens up a world of possibilities for growth and success.

Common Professional Challenges and How Responsibility Can Help

Let's explore some common challenges that people face in their careers and how taking responsibility can help address them.

1. Stagnation and Lack of Growth

Many people find themselves stuck in a job where they don't see any growth opportunities. They might feel like they're just going through the motions, doing the same tasks day after day, with no clear path forward.

Taking responsibility for your career growth means actively seeking out development opportunities. This might involve taking on new projects, pursuing additional training or education, or even seeking out a mentor who can help guide you. Don't wait for your employer to offer you opportunities—create them yourself. By taking ownership of your growth, you can move out of stagnation and start advancing in your career.

2. Handling Mistakes and Failures

Mistakes and failures are inevitable in any career. Whether it's a project that didn't go as planned or a decision that backfired, everyone faces setbacks at some point. How you handle these situations can make or break your career.

Taking responsibility for your mistakes means owning up to them, learning from them, and taking steps to make things right. Face them head-on instead of trying to shift the blame or cover up your errors. This approach helps you grow and builds trust with your colleagues and supervisors. When you demonstrate that you can handle setbacks with maturity and accountability, you position yourself as a leader who can be relied upon in difficult situations.

3. Navigating Office Politics
Office politics can be one of the most challenging aspects of professional life. Navigating relationships with colleagues, dealing with competition, and managing conflicts can be tricky, especially in a high-stakes environment.

Taking responsibility in a political environment means maintaining your integrity, staying true to your values, and being mindful of how your actions affect others. It involves being strategic in your interactions, building positive relationships, and addressing conflicts constructively. By taking responsibility for engaging with office politics, you can navigate these challenges gracefully and professionally rather than getting caught up in negativity or drama.

4. Balancing Work and Personal Life
Many professionals struggle to find the right balance between work and personal life. When work demands become overwhelming, it can be challenging to maintain

that balance, leading to stress and burnout.

Taking responsibility for your work-life balance means setting boundaries, managing your time effectively, and prioritising your well-being. It involves recognising when to step back and recharge and being proactive in creating a healthy balance between your professional and personal life. Taking ownership of this aspect of your career can prevent burnout and maintain your overall well-being.

Practical Steps to Take Professional Responsibility

Now that we've explored the importance of professional responsibility and how it can help you overcome common challenges, let's look at some practical steps you can take to start thriving in your career.

1. Set Clear Career Goals
Setting clear goals is the first step to taking responsibility for your career. What do you want to achieve in your career? Where do you see yourself in the next year, five or ten years? Having clear goals gives you direction and helps you make intentional decisions about your career path. Please write down your goals, break them into actionable steps, and regularly review your progress.

2. Seek Out Opportunities for Growth
Don't wait for opportunities to come to you—seek them out. Look for ways to expand your skills, take on new challenges, and gain more experience. This might involve volunteering for projects, pursuing additional training or education, or finding a mentor to guide you. By being proactive in your growth, you position yourself for more

tremendous success.

3. Own Your Mistakes and Learn from Them

Everyone makes mistakes, but how you handle them is what matters. When you make a mistake, own it. Acknowledge what went wrong, take steps to fix it, and reflect on what you can learn from the experience. This approach helps you grow and builds trust with your colleagues and supervisors.

4. Build Positive Relationships

Strong professional relationships are critical to a successful career. Take responsibility for interacting with others—be respectful, supportive, and collaborative. Build positive relationships with your colleagues, supervisors, and mentors. These connections can provide valuable support, guidance, and opportunities throughout your career.

5. Manage Your Time and Prioritize Your Well-Being

Taking responsibility for your career also means managing your time effectively and prioritising your well-being. Set boundaries, plan your time wisely, and ensure you care for yourself physically and mentally. A healthy work-life balance is crucial for long-term success and fulfilment.

THE LEGACY OF RATAN TATA: PROFESSIONAL RESPONSIBILITY IN LEADERSHIP

To understand the true essence of professional responsibility, we must reflect on the life of Ratan Tata, one of India's most respected and visionary business leaders, who passed away on September 9, 2024. His journey is a testament to how taking responsibility in one's professional role can transform industries, impact communities, and leave a lasting legacy.

The company was at a critical point when Ratan Tata took over the Tata Group in 1991. The world was changing, and Tata Group needed to evolve to stay relevant in an increasingly competitive global market. Ratan Tata's leadership wasn't just about achieving financial success; it was deeply rooted in ethical responsibility, innovation, and serving the greater good. His decisions were always guided by a deep sense of duty to shareholders and society.

One of the most iconic moments of Ratan Tata's career came during the development of the Tata Nano. In the mid-2000s, Tata envisioned creating an affordable, safe, and reliable car for the masses. At the time, millions of Indian families travelled precariously on two-wheelers, often crammed onto scooters in unsafe conditions. Ratan Tata saw this and wanted to provide a solution—an affordable car that could bring safety and dignity to these families. The Tata Nano, dubbed "the people's car," was his bold response to this challenge.

Developing the world's cheapest car came with immense challenges. There were widespread doubts about whether Tata could produce a car cheaply without compromising safety and quality. But Ratan Tata's vision never wavered. He oversaw the project, ensuring the car met safety standards while remaining affordable. His leadership exemplified professional responsibility at its finest—putting people's needs at the forefront while challenging the norms of the industry.

Although the Nano failed commercially, Ratan Tata stood by the project. He took full responsibility, acknowledging the marketing missteps, but never regretted the vision behind it. The Nano symbolized more than just a car; it demonstrated his commitment to creating solutions for real problems. Even facing challenges, Ratan Tata's unwavering dedication to social good over mere profit defined his professional philosophy.

Another poignant example of Ratan Tata's professional responsibility came during the tragic 26/11 terrorist attacks on the Taj Mahal Palace Hotel, owned by the Tata Group. The attack left many dead and wounded, including employees and guests of the hotel. While the world watched in horror, Ratan Tata responded with compassion and responsibility far beyond business. He visited the victims' families and ensured that the Tata Group provided long-term financial and medical support to all affected. His leadership in the aftermath of that tragedy showed that professional responsibility isn't just about managing a company—it's about standing with people in their darkest moments and caring for those who have trusted you.

Ratan Tata has embodied humility, integrity, and a deep sense of responsibility throughout his life. Even after stepping down as chairman of Tata Group in 2012, he remained influential, using his voice to advocate for ethical business practices and societal development. His guiding principle was always clear: businesses exist not just for profits but for the betterment of society.

With his passing, India and the world lost a giant of industry and leadership. But Ratan Tata's legacy is far from over. His life is a reminder that professional responsibility is not just about doing well in business—it's about doing good in the world. His choices reshaped industries, improved countless lives, and set a standard for ethical leadership that will be remembered for generations.

Ratan Tata's story is one of quiet but profound impact, demonstrating that the accurate measure of leadership lies not in what you achieve for yourself but in the legacy you leave behind for others. His life is a powerful example of professional responsibility: the courage to take bold risks, the humility to learn from setbacks, and the unwavering commitment to prioritize the greater good.

Even though he is no longer with us, Ratan Tata's values will continue to inspire those who seek to lead with integrity, compassion, and responsibility.

Taking Control of Your Career
Your career is one of the most significant aspects of your life, and taking responsibility for it is crucial to your success and fulfilment. In this chapter, we've explored what it means to accept professional responsibility, why it's essential, and how to start thriving in your career by embracing this mindset.

I encourage you to reflect on your career and consider how to take responsibility for your growth, actions, and future. Your career is in your hands, and by owning it, you empower yourself to create the professional life you desire.

CHAPTER SEVEN

Mastering Money: Owning Your Financial Future

You and your spouse work hard—managing demanding jobs, juggling kids' school fees, household expenses, and those inevitable unplanned emergencies. Yet, the budget seems to fall apart by the middle of the month. The electricity bill arrives higher than expected, a wedding to attend, or your child's tuition demands an extra payment.

No matter how much you try to save, something always comes up. Discussions about money turn into heated debates: "Why did we buy that new appliance?" or "Do we need to order food so often?" The stress isn't just about the money—it's about feeling like you're losing control of something essential to your family's stability and future.

But what if you could change this pattern? What if you could take charge of your finances, ensuring every penny has a purpose? Financial responsibility isn't about earning more; it's about managing smarter. By taking ownership, you can move from chaos to clarity, creating a secure future for your family.

Financial responsibility isn't just about paying bills on time or ensuring you have enough money for daily expenses. It's about understanding your relationship with money, controlling your financial decisions, and planning for your present and future. When you take responsibility for your finances, you empower yourself to build a stable, secure, and independent financial life.

At its core, financial responsibility is about being accountable for how you manage your money. It's not just about making ends meet—it's about understanding your financial habits, making conscious decisions, and planning for the future. Financial responsibility means knowing where your money is going, living within your means, saving for emergencies and future goals, and making informed financial decisions.

Many people shy away from financial responsibility because money can feel overwhelming or intimidating. But here's the thing: avoiding your finances doesn't make the problems disappear. It often makes things worse. Taking responsibility for your finances, on the other hand, gives you control. It empowers you to make choices that align with your values, goals, and long-term plans.

Why Financial Responsibility is Important

1. It Reduces Stress and Anxiety
Money is one of the leading causes of stress for people. When you're constantly worried about paying bills,

managing debt, or not having enough for the future, it takes a toll on your mental and emotional well-being. Taking responsibility for your finances helps reduce this stress because it puts you in control. Instead of being reactive and scrambling to manage your money, you become proactive in planning, budgeting, and saving. This gives you peace of mind and a sense of security.

2. It Leads to Greater Independence

When you're financially responsible, you gain independence. You no longer rely on others for financial support, and you can make choices that align with your values and goals. Financial freedom allows you to take risks, pursue opportunities, and live life on your terms without worrying about money holding you back.

3. It Helps You Build a Secure Future

Financial responsibility isn't just about the present—it's about the future. By managing your money wisely today, you're setting yourself up for long-term success. Whether you're saving for retirement, buying a home, or achieving other financial goals, being responsible with your money ensures you're prepared for whatever life throws your way.

Let's understand some common financial challenges many face and how taking responsibility can help you overcome them.

1. Living Beyond Your Means

One of the most common financial struggles is living beyond one's means—spending more money than one earns. This often leads to debt, stress, and an inability to save for the future. Spending on things you want now can be tempting, but when your expenses consistently exceed your income, it becomes a problem.—spending while spending

Taking responsibility for your spending habits is the first step toward living within your means. This means being honest with yourself about where your money is going and adjusting your spending with your income. Creating a budget is a great way to track expenses and ensure you live within your means. It helps you prioritise your needs over wants and gives you a clear picture of your available money for saving, investing, and other financial goals.

2. Accumulating Debt

Debt can be overwhelming, especially when constantly trying to catch up on payments. Whether credit card debt, student loans, or car payments, accumulating debt can create a cycle of financial stress that's hard to break free from.

Taking responsibility for your debt means facing it head-on rather than avoiding it. This involves understanding how much debt you have, creating a plan to pay it off, and avoiding taking on new debt unless it's an absolutely necessity. Prioritising high-interest debt and making consistent payments can help you get out of debt faster and reduce the financial burden. It's also important to understand the root causes of your debt and make changes to avoid falling into the same patterns in the future.

3. Lack of Emergency Savings

Life is full of unexpected expenses—a medical emergency, car repair, or sudden job loss. These unexpected costs can throw your entire financial plan off course without an emergency fund, leading to stress or debt.

Building an emergency fund is a vital part of financial responsibility. Start by setting aside a small amount each month to save enough to cover 3 to 6 months' living expenses. This safety net gives you peace of mind and ensures you're prepared for whatever life throws. Even if you can only save a little initially, prioritising savings is essential to financial security.

4. Not Planning for the Future
It's easy to get caught up in managing your finances daily and forget to plan for the future. Whether saving for retirement, investing in your long-term goals, or preparing for major life events, failing to plan can leave you unprepared and financially vulnerable later in life.

Taking responsibility for your future means being proactive in your financial planning. Start by setting long-term financial goals—whether saving for a down payment on a house, investing for retirement, or planning for your children's education. Once you have clear goals, create a plan to achieve them. This might involve contributing to a retirement account, setting up an investment portfolio, or increasing your monthly savings. Planning for the future gives you a sense of direction and ensures you're prepared for the years ahead.

Now that we've explored the importance of financial responsibility and how it can help you overcome common challenges, let's look at some practical steps you can take to start taking control of your finances.

1. Create a Budget and Stick to It

A budget is the foundation of financial responsibility. It helps you track your income and expenses, ensuring you live within your means and make intentional financial decisions. Start by listing all your sources of income and monthly expenses, including fixed costs (like rent, credit card, and loan payments) and variable costs (like groceries or entertainment). Once you have a clear picture of where your money is going, make adjustments to ensure that your spending aligns with your financial goals.

2. Build an Emergency Fund

An emergency fund is essential for financial security. Aim to save enough to cover at least 3 to 6 months of living expenses. This fund should be easily accessible in an emergency but kept separate from your regular checking account to avoid temptation. Start small, even if it's just setting aside a few dollars each week, and gradually build your emergency fund over time.

3. Pay Off High-Interest Debt

High-interest debt, like credit card debt, can quickly become a financial burden. Make a plan to pay off this debt as soon as possible. Start by prioritising the debt with the highest interest rate, and make more than the minimum payment if possible. Once you've paid off one debt, move on to the next one. Avoid taking on new debt unless necessary, and focus on paying off what you owe.

4. Save for Long-Term Goals

Saving for long-term goals, whether retirement, buying a home, or investing in your education, is essential to financial responsibility. Set clear financial goals for the future and create a plan to achieve them. This might involve contributing to a retirement account, setting up a savings plan for a major purchase, or investing in stocks or other assets. The earlier you start saving, the more time your money has to grow.

5. Make Informed Financial Decisions
Being financially responsible means making informed decisions about how you manage your money. Before making major financial decisions, take the time to research your options, understand the potential risks and benefits, and consider how each choice aligns with your long-term goals. Whether you're deciding on a major purchase, taking out a loan, or investing in a new opportunity, being informed helps you make smart, responsible choices.

THE STORY OF AMITABH BACHCHAN: FINANCIAL RESPONSIBILITY AND RECOVERY

Amitabh Bachchan, known as the Shahenshah of Bollywood, is celebrated for his unmatched charisma and legendary career. But beyond the glitz and glamour lies an inspiring story of resilience, financial responsibility, and the sheer determination to rebuild a life when everything seemed to collapse.

In the late 1990s, Amitabh Bachchan faced one of the darkest phases of his life. His production company, Amitabh Bachchan Corporation Ltd. (ABCL), which aimed to produce films, manage events, and promote talent, suffered massive losses. Poor investments, mismanagement, and market missteps led the company into a financial crisis. ABCL was burdened with a debt of over ₹90 crores, and creditors were knocking on his doors. The superstar who had once ruled the box office now faced public humiliation, lawsuits, and the possibility of losing everything, including his family home.

Amitabh described this period as one in which he felt completely lost, unable to see a way out. He was in his mid-50s, an age many consider settling into the twilight years of their careers. The financial crisis was not just about money—it attacked his dignity, reputation, and self-worth.

Instead of succumbing to despair, Amitabh Bachchan chose to take full responsibility for the situation. He didn't shy away from the challenges or try to shift the blame onto others. Instead, he boldly decided to face his debts and rebuild from scratch.

The first step he took was to acknowledge the reality of his situation. He assessed his financial mess and began strategizing ways to repay his debts. Amitabh decided to return to the one thing he knew best: acting. Despite his age and the uncertainties of the film industry, he approached producers and directors for work. Given his towering status, his humility in doing so was a testament to his resolve.

Amitabh didn't just take any work; he carefully chose projects that would allow him to repay his debts while rebuilding his image. One pivotal moment in his comeback was his role in the film Mohabbatein (2000), in which he shared the screen with rising superstar Shah Rukh Khan. The role was a departure from his typical angry young man persona, showcasing his versatility and earning him widespread acclaim.

Around the same time, he took a calculated risk by becoming the host of Kaun Banega Crorepati (KBC), the Indian adaptation of Who Wants to Be a Millionaire? Many questioned why a superstar of his stature would venture into television, which was then considered a step down from films. But Amitabh saw the potential. The show was an instant hit, connecting him to audiences across generations and bringing him back into the spotlight. The success of KBC not only revived his finances but also solidified his position as a beloved cultural icon.

Amitabh Bachchan approached his financial recovery with discipline and focus. Every rupee he earned was directed toward repaying his debts. He made significant lifestyle adjustments, cutting unnecessary expenses and prioritizing financial stability over extravagance.

He also demonstrated remarkable patience and resilience. Repaying a debt as massive as ₹90 crores was no overnight feat—it required years of consistent effort, strategic choices, and unwavering dedication. Over time, his hard work paid off, and he successfully cleared all his debts, regaining his financial independence and stability.

Lessons in Financial Responsibility

1. Facing Reality: Amitabh didn't run from his problems or deny their existence. He acknowledged the crisis and took responsibility for finding solutions.

2. Returning to Strengths: By going back to acting, Amitabh

leveraged his core skills to generate income and rebuild his career.

3. Adaptability: His decision to host KBC showed his willingness to adapt to new opportunities and embrace unconventional paths.

4. Discipline: Amitabh's disciplined approach to managing earnings and prioritizing debt repayment was key to his recovery.

5. Resilience and Humility: Despite the setbacks, he maintained his dignity, worked tirelessly, and never lost sight of his goals.

Today, Amitabh Bachchan is a revered actor and a symbol of resilience and financial accountability. His story powerfully reminds us that no matter how dire a situation may seem, taking responsibility and working with focus and determination can turn things around.

Amitabh's journey offers valuable lessons: taking responsibility doesn't mean the absence of setbacks—it means facing those setbacks with courage, learning from them, and taking consistent action to rise again. Amitabh's example proves that recovery is always possible when you embrace responsibility and never give up, whether managing personal finances, navigating a career setback, or rebuilding after failure.

Body and Mind Balance: The Ultimate Responsibility

Let me take you through what a typical day used to look like for me. My alarm would buzz at 6:30 AM, but I'd hit snooze at least twice. By the time I got up, I'd already be running late. Breakfast? Usually skipped. I'd grab a quick cup of tea and rush to the office, mentally making a list of everything that needed to get done. Lunch was whatever was convenient—often something oily or fried, eaten at my desk while I replied to emails. By the end of the day, I'd be exhausted but still convince myself to push through a few more tasks. Dinner was rushed, and then I'd collapse into bed, scrolling through my phone until I fell asleep.

This routine felt normal—like what every working professional deals with. I thought I was managing just fine. But slowly, it started to catch up with me. I'd wake up feeling groggy, struggle to focus during meetings, and constantly rely on caffeine to get through the day. Stress was my constant companion, and my body sent me signals

I was too busy to notice—frequent headaches, low energy, and even minor aches and pains that I brushed aside.

Then, one day, everything came to a head. I woke up feeling completely drained, both physically and mentally. My body felt heavy, my thoughts were foggy, and for the first time, I couldn't push through the day like I always had. My body had hit the brakes and refused to move forward until I paid attention.

That day, I realized I had been living on autopilot—so focused on work and responsibilities that I had completely neglected my health. The irony? My productivity, which I thought I was preserving by skipping meals, pushing through exhaustion, and avoiding rest, had taken a nosedive. I wasn't performing at my best because I wasn't caring for myself.

It was a wake-up call that forced me to reevaluate everything. I started making small but deliberate changes. I began prioritizing simple yet nutritious breakfasts to fuel my mornings. I carved out 20 minutes a day for a walk, even if it was just around the office block. I committed to shutting off work at a reasonable hour to give myself time to unwind before bed.

The changes weren't easy at first. I had to break old habits and remind myself daily that taking care of my health wasn't selfish but necessary. But over time, the results were undeniable. I felt more energetic, my focus improved, and even the stress I used to carry around started to feel manageable. The best part? My work benefited, too. I was more creative, efficient, and better equipped to handle challenges.

If you're reading this and see glimpses of your routine, let me tell you: it doesn't have to be this way. Taking responsibility for your health isn't about perfection but progress. It's about realizing that everything else in your life gets better when you take care of your body and mind. You have more energy, clarity, and resilience to face whatever comes your way.

I'm sharing this story because I know how easy it is to think that health can be put on the back burner. But the truth is, when you care for your body and mind, everything else in your life improves. You have more energy, clarity, and resilience. You can handle stress, take on challenges, and enjoy life more fully.

Your health is the foundation upon which everything else is built. When your body and mind are functioning well, you have the energy, focus, and emotional stability to handle whatever comes your way. But when you neglect your health, it doesn't take long for things to start falling apart.

Think about it: how well can you perform at work if you're constantly tired, stressed, or physically uncomfortable? How much can you enjoy time with your family or friends if you're always feeling anxious or overwhelmed? Your physical and mental health aren't separate from the rest of your life—they're deeply connected to everything you do.

Here's why taking responsibility for your health matters:

1. Increased Energy and Focus

When you take care of your body—by eating well, staying active, and getting enough rest—you have more energy to get through your day. You can focus better, think more clearly, and be more productive. Your brain needs fuel just as much as your body, and when you give it what it needs, you'll notice a massive difference in how you perform.

2. Better Stress Management

Life is full of stressors, and while we can't always control what happens to us, we can control how we respond. Taking responsibility for your mental well-being makes you better equipped to handle stress healthily. Regular exercise, proper sleep, mindfulness, and even taking breaks can help you manage stress before it affects your health.

3. Long-Term Health and Prevention

Taking care of yourself now isn't just about feeling good in the moment—it's about preventing bigger health problems. By maintaining a healthy lifestyle, you reduce your risk of developing chronic illnesses like heart disease, diabetes, and depression. It's about playing the long game, ensuring you survive and thrive for years.

One of the biggest lessons I've learned on this journey is that physical and mental health are deeply connected. You can't separate the two. When your body feels good, your mind is sharper, clearer, and more positive. When you care for your mental health, you're more likely to make better decisions about your physical health.

For example, I felt less stressed and more focused when I exercised regularly. Physical activity improved my body and helped clear my mind. Similarly, when I started practising mindfulness and managing my stress better, I was more motivated to take care of my physical health. It's a cycle—each aspect of health feeds into the other.

Now that we've explored why health is so important let's talk about how you can start taking responsibility for your well-being. Here are some practical steps that helped me and can help you, too:

1. Prioritize Sleep

If one thing can make or break your health, it's sleep. I could function on five or six hours of sleep a night for a long time, but I was wrong. Sleep is when your body repairs, your brain processes information, and your energy is restored. Without enough sleep, everything starts to fall apart—your mood, focus, and immune system.

Start by making sleep a priority. Aim for 7-9 hours of quality sleep each night, and establish a bedtime routine that helps you unwind. This meant turning off screens an hour before bed, reading something relaxing, and sticking to a consistent sleep schedule. It made a world of difference.

2. Move Your Body Every Day

You don't have to be a fitness fanatic to benefit from regular movement. Exercise isn't just about losing weight or building muscle—it's about keeping your body functioning well. Even something as simple as a daily walk can boost your mood, improve your cardiovascular health, and help you manage stress.

I started small by incorporating short walks into my day, and as I got more comfortable, I added yoga. Find what works for you and make it a habit. Your body will thank you.

3. Eat for Energy and Health

I used to eat whatever was convenient—fast food, snacks, and lots of coffee to keep me going. But once I started paying attention to my eating, I realised how much better I felt when I fuelled my body with nutritious foods.

Focus on eating whole foods that give you sustained energy, like fruits, vegetables, lean proteins, and whole grains. Avoid relying on sugar or caffeine to get you through the day. You don't need to be perfect—aim for balance and make choices that support your long-term health.

4. Manage Stress Mindfully

Stress is inevitable, but how you manage it makes all the difference. I used to let stress build up until it overwhelmed me, but now I take a more proactive approach. I practice mindfulness, take regular breaks during the day, and make time for activities that relax and recharge me.

If you're stressed, try incorporating mindfulness techniques like deep breathing or meditation. It doesn't have to be complicated—just taking a few moments to focus on your breath can help calm your mind and body.

5. Make Time for Mental Health

Mental health is just as important as physical health, which we must take seriously. Whether it's managing stress, dealing with anxiety, or simply making time for self-care, mental well-being should be a priority.

For me, making time for mental health meant setting boundaries at work, saying no when I needed to, and seeking support when things felt overwhelming. It also meant making time for hobbies and activities that brought me joy. Don't hesitate to reach out to a therapist or counsellor if you need help—there's no shame in taking care of your mind.

My Turning Point: Learning to Balance Health and Life
I'll never forget when I realised that taking care of my health wasn't optional but essential. After my body forced me to slow down, I had to confront the fact that I had been neglecting myself for far too long. It wasn't just about working hard anymore—it was about working smart, which meant taking care of my most important asset: my body and mind.

Once I made that shift, everything else in my life started to improve. My energy levels increased, my mood stabilised, and I became more productive at work. I was able to show up for the people in my life in a more meaningful way because I wasn't constantly running on empty. I learned that when you take responsibility for your health, you're not just doing it for yourself but for everyone around you, too.

Start small. Commit to one healthy habit today—eating a proper meal, drinking more water, or just stepping outside for a few minutes to breathe. Trust me, the ripple effect will surprise you. Taking responsibility for your health is the best investment you can make—not just for yourself, but for the people and dreams that matter most to you.

Your health is the foundation for everything else in your life. Without it, even the best opportunities and experiences can feel overwhelming or out of reach. Taking responsibility for your physical and mental well-being gives you the tools to live a more energised, fulfilling, and balanced life.

I've shared my learning journey to prioritise health and well-being, and I hope it resonates with you. It's never too late to start making healthier choices. Whether getting more sleep, eating better, managing stress, or simply moving your body more, every small step you take adds up.

How are you currently taking care of your health, and where can you make changes? Your body and mind deserve the best care you can give them, and by taking responsibility, you're setting yourself up for long-term success and happiness.

CHAPTER NINE

Ripple Effect: How You Can Change the World by Changing Yourself

For a long time, I believed that my life was entirely about me—my goals, my work, and my happiness. It wasn't that I didn't care about others, but I thought that as long as I was doing my part, the world around me would somehow figure itself out. But over time, I realised that life isn't lived in isolation. We're all part of a larger community, whether that's our neighbourhood, workplace, or even the world as a whole. The more I connected with that idea, the more I understood the importance of taking responsibility not just for my own life but for the well-being of others around me, too.

Taking responsibility within your community doesn't mean you have to solve the world's problems alone. It's about recognising that you have the power to make a difference, no matter how small your actions may seem. Social responsibility is a key part of living a fulfilling and meaningful life, whether it's helping a neighbour in need, volunteering your time, or simply being more conscious of how your decisions impact others.

I'll never forget the first time I realised how much of an impact I could make by simply showing up for others. It wasn't something grand or world-changing, but it was one of those moments that stuck with me.

Several years ago, I volunteered at a local community centre that ran after-school programs for kids. I wasn't sure what to expect, but I figured I'd help out a few hours a week, maybe help with homework or play games with the kids. I didn't expect a sense of purpose and connection from being part of something bigger than myself.

One boy, Rohan, was struggling. He had trouble focusing, often seemed frustrated, and fell behind in his schoolwork. At first, I wasn't sure how to help him—I wasn't a teacher or an education expert. However, I decided to sit with him during homework and see what we could do together. As the weeks went by, I noticed something shift in Rohan. It wasn't that he suddenly became a star student, but he started to trust that someone was there for him, that someone cared. We worked through his frustrations and celebrated small victories, and by the end of the school year, he had improved not only in his schoolwork but in his confidence. It was a small change, but it mattered to him—and it mattered to me.

That experience taught me that you don't have to be a superhero to make a difference in your community. Sometimes, the most meaningful impact comes from consistently showing up, offering support, and being willing to connect with others. It's about taking responsibility for how your presence, actions, and choices affect the world around you.

So why is social responsibility so important?
Why should we care about contributing to our communities and helping others?

Here's what I've learned over the years:

1. It Creates Connection and Belonging
Humans are social creatures, and we all crave connection. When you engage with your community, you build relationships with others who share your environment, challenges, and aspirations. Being part of a community gives you a sense of belonging and reminds you that you're not alone in this world. When you take responsibility for helping others, you strengthen those bonds and create a more supportive and connected environment for everyone.

2. It Gives Life Greater Meaning
There's something incredibly fulfilling about knowing that you've positively impacted someone else's life. When you step outside of your concerns and focus on the needs of others, you gain a sense of purpose beyond personal success. Helping others benefits the community and enriches your life by giving you a deeper sense of meaning and fulfilment.

3. It Makes the World a Better Place
It might sound cliché, but it's true: when we all take responsibility for contributing to the well-being of our communities, the world becomes a better place. Even small actions—like picking up litter, supporting a local business,

or mentoring a young person—can have a ripple effect that spreads far beyond what we can see. By choosing to act with kindness, generosity, and responsibility, you help create a more compassionate and just society.

My Journey to Taking Social Responsibility Seriously

There was another turning point in my life that reinforced my commitment to social responsibility. It wasn't planned, but it made me rethink how I approached my role in the world. I was travelling for work and staying in a new city. One evening, I decided to explore the area by foot. Walking through the streets, I noticed a small group of homeless people huddled under a bridge. It was clear that they were struggling to stay warm on that cold evening.

I'd seen homelessness before, but something about that moment hit me. I had just come from a nice hotel, a warm meal, and here were people who didn't even have the basic necessities to get through the night. I kept walking, but I couldn't shake the feeling that I needed to do anything to help.

That evening, I went to a nearby store, bought some blankets, and returned to the bridge to hand them out. It wasn't much, but it was something. As I handed the blankets to the group, I realised this wasn't about "saving" anyone but acknowledging their humanity and showing that someone cared. That simple act of kindness didn't change their circumstances but created a moment of connection and compassion.

Since that night, I've made it a point to look for meaningful ways to contribute to my community. Whether it's through volunteering, donating, or simply being more mindful of the people around me, I've learned that taking responsibility for the well-being of others isn't just about charity—it's about building a world where we all feel valued and supported.

If you're wondering how you can start taking responsibility for your community, here are some practical steps that have helped me, and that can help you make a positive impact:

1. Get Involved Locally
One of the best ways to take responsibility for your community is to get involved in local initiatives. Whether volunteering at a food bank, participating in neighbourhood clean-up efforts, or joining a regional organisation, there are plenty of ways to make a difference right where you live. The key is to start small and find something that resonates with you. Over time, you'll build connections and discover how to contribute best.

2. Be a Good Neighbour
Sometimes, social responsibility is as simple as being a good neighbour. Offer to help someone with their groceries, check in on an elderly neighbour, or lend a hand when someone is in need. These small acts of kindness may seem insignificant, but they create a sense of community and trust that makes life better for everyone.

3. Support Local Businesses
Supporting local businesses is another way to contribute to your community. By shopping locally, you're helping to sustain the livelihoods of the people around you. Small

businesses are the backbone of many communities, and by choosing to spend your money locally, you're helping to create jobs, support families, and keep your community thriving.

4. Advocate for Causes You Care About
Social responsibility can also mean using your voice to advocate for causes that matter to you. Whether it's environmental sustainability, social justice, or education, countless issues need attention. You don't have to be an expert or a leader to make a difference—sometimes, simply spreading awareness or joining a movement can create real change.

5. Be Mindful of Your Impact
Lastly, take responsibility for how your actions impact others directly and indirectly. This could mean being mindful of how much waste you produce, how you treat others in your daily interactions, or how your decisions affect the environment. By being conscious of your impact, you can make choices that align with your values and contribute to the greater good.

The Ripple Effect: How Small Actions Lead to Big Change

One of the most powerful lessons about social responsibility is the ripple effect. Often, we underestimate the impact of small actions, thinking that they don't make a difference in the grand scheme of things. But I've seen repeatedly that even the most minor acts of kindness, generosity, or responsibility can create ripples that spread far beyond what we initially imagined.

Think about when someone did something small for you—a kind word, a helping hand, a moment of understanding. How did that make you feel? How did it change your day or even your perspective? Those small acts matter; when we each take responsibility for spreading positivity and care, we create a ripple effect that can lead to lasting change.

Social responsibility isn't just about grand gestures or solving global problems—it's about recognizing that each of us has the power to make a difference in our communities. Whether it's through volunteering, advocating for causes, or simply being kind and mindful in our daily interactions, we can all contribute to building a more compassionate and connected world.

Remember, you don't have to do everything—just start with what you can do. The ripple effect of your actions can spread farther than you ever imagined.

CHAPTER TEN

The Ultimate Power Play: Owning Every Part of Your Life

Imagine standing at the end of your life, looking back, and knowing that you gave everything you had—that no dream was left unchased, no potential untapped, and no part of your life left to chance. In his transformative book Die Empty, Todd Henry challenges us to pour our best work, ideas, and energy into each day so that when we leave this world, we do so with nothing left undone. This chapter is about embracing that philosophy—about taking full ownership of every aspect of your life so you can live fully, purposefully, and without regret.

Owning every part of your life is the ultimate power play. It's about saying, "I am responsible for my choices, my actions, and my outcomes." It's a declaration that you won't leave your success, happiness, or fulfilment to chance or others. It's about stepping into your life with intention, courage, and an unwavering commitment to make the most of the time you've been given.

The Wake-Up Call: Facing the Clock

Time is the great equalizer. No matter who you are or where you're from, we all have the same 24 hours in a day. But how we choose to spend those hours is what sets us apart. Too often, we go through life on autopilot—chasing deadlines, managing daily chaos, and putting off the things that truly matter. We tell ourselves there will be time to write that book, start that business, mend that relationship, or take care of our health later. But what if later never comes?

I remember a moment in my career when I was juggling multiple responsibilities—work projects, family commitments, and personal goals—and kept pushing to the sidelines. It felt like I was always busy but wasn't making real progress. Then, one day, someone said, "The graveyard is the richest place on Earth because it's where all the unfulfilled dreams, unwritten books, and unlaunched ideas go to die."

That thought hit me like a thunderbolt. I realized I was holding back—not because I lacked time, but because I wasn't owning every part of my life. I was waiting for perfect conditions to act, and in doing so, I was letting valuable opportunities slip away. That's when I decided: No more waiting. The buck stops with me.

Why Ownership is the Ultimate Power Play

Owning your life doesn't mean controlling everything—because, let's face it, some things are beyond your control. But it does mean taking full responsibility for responding to the events, challenges, and opportunities life throws your way. It's about recognizing that you are the common denominator in every area of your life and that your choices shape your reality.

Here's why ownership is so powerful:

1. It Liberates You
When you take ownership, you free yourself from the blame game. You stop waiting for others to change or for circumstances to align. Instead, you focus on what you can do. This shift in mindset is liberating—it puts the power back in your hands.

2. It Amplifies Your Impact
When you own your life, you bring your full self to every situation. You stop holding back your ideas, energy, and potential. This commitment to showing up fully amplifies your impact at work, in relationships, and in the community.

3. It Leaves a Legacy
Owning your life means living intentionally for today and the future you want to create. It's about leaving behind something meaningful—the lives you've touched, the projects you've built, or the example you've set for others.

So, how do you move from living reactively to owning every part of your life? Here are some steps to get you started:

1. Clarify Your Values and Priorities
Ask yourself: What truly matters to me? When you're clear

on your values and priorities, making decisions and aligning your actions with your goals becomes easier. This meant prioritizing meaningful work, nurturing relationships, and investing in my health and personal growth.

2. Audit Your Time
Take a hard look at how you're spending your time. Are you dedicating your energy to the things that matter most, or are you getting caught up in distractions? Time is your most valuable resource—spend it wisely.

3. Take Bold Action
Stop waiting for the perfect moment to act—it doesn't exist. Whether it's launching a project, pursuing a passion, or having a difficult conversation, take the first step today. Bold action, even in small increments, creates momentum and builds confidence.

4. Embrace Responsibility for Every Role
You're not just a professional, a parent, or a friend—you're all of these and more. Taking ownership means showing up fully in each role you play. It means asking, "What can I do to improve this relationship, this project, or this situation?"

5. Learn from Failure
Ownership doesn't mean perfection—it means accountability. When things don't go as planned, own your mistakes, learn from them, and move forward. Each failure is a stepping stone to growth.

Taking ownership of your life isn't just about achieving success—it's about living fully. It's about pouring your energy, talents, and passion into everything you do, so that when your time comes, you leave nothing undone. You don't want to look back and wonder, "What if I had tried harder? What if I had taken that risk? What if I had given more of myself?"

Living this way doesn't mean you'll never face challenges or setbacks. It means you'll face them with courage, knowing you've done everything you can to live intentionally and authentically. You'll know that you didn't hold back your best work, your love, or your ideas.

Here's the ultimate question I want you to ask yourself: "What do I need to own today to live fully tomorrow?" Is it a project you've been procrastinating on? A relationship that needs mending? A habit you need to break? Whatever it is, take responsibility for it—because the buck stops with you.

When you take full ownership of your life, you're not just living for the present—you're shaping your legacy. And that, my friend, is the ultimate power play. Make it count.